Adding and subtracting 5–6

Author: Lynn Huggins-Cooper
Illustrator: Emma Holt and Chris McGhie

How to use this book

Look out for these features!

IN THE ACTIVITIES

The parents' notes at the top of each activity will give you:
- ► a simple explanation about what your child is learni
- ► an idea of how you can work with your child on the activity.

This small page number guides you to the back of the book, where you will find further ideas for help.

These magic stars provide useful facts and helpful hints

AT THE BACK OF THE BOOK

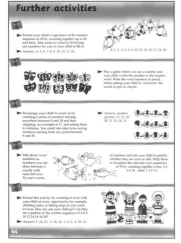

Every activity has a section for parents containing:
- ► further explanations about what the activity teaches
- ► games that can be easily recreated at home
- ► questions to ask your child to encourage their learnir
- ► tips on varying the activity if it seems too easy or too difficult for your child.

You will also find the answers at the back of the book.

HELPING YOUR CHILD AS THEY USE THIS BOOK

Why not try starting at the beginning of the book and work through it? Your child should only attempt one activity at a time. Remember, it is best to learn little and often when we are feeling wide awake!

EQUIPMENT YOUR CHILD WILL NEED

- ► a pencil for writing
- ► an eraser for correcting mistakes
- ► coloured pencils for drawing and colouring in.

You might also like to have ready some spare paper and some collections of objects (for instance, small toys, Lego bricks, buttons...) for some of the activities.

Contents

Counting to 20

Fill in the missing numbers.

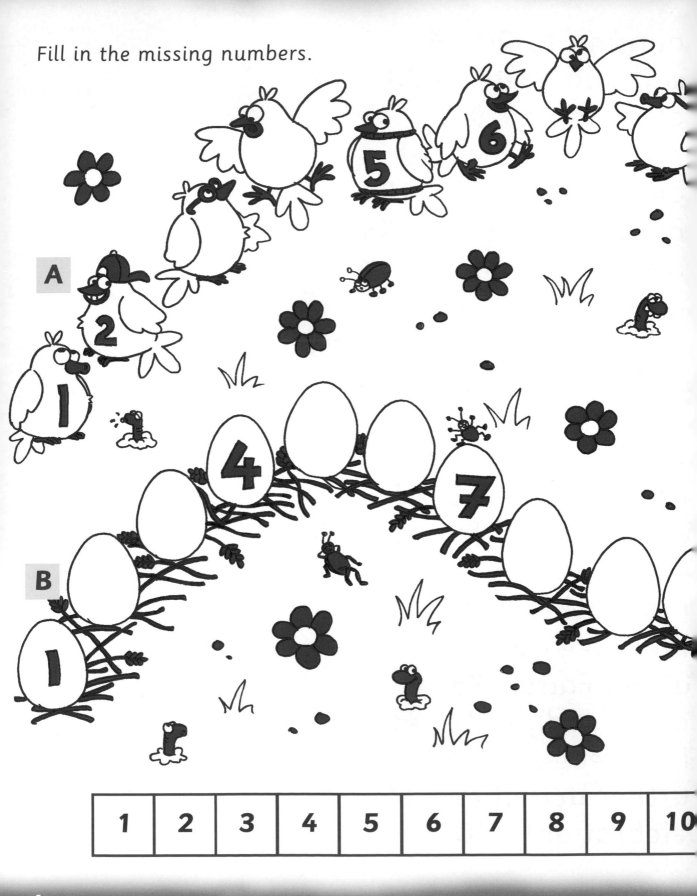

| 1 | 2 | 3 | 4 | 5 | 6 | 7 | 8 | 9 | 10 |

4

This activity will help your child to learn the sequence of numbers to 20.

Read the numbers on the birds together, then fill in the missing numbers. Point to the number line, if necessary.

| 11 | 12 | 13 | 14 | 15 | 16 | 17 | 18 | 19 | 20 |

Read and write to 20

Look at these numbers. Copy them in the boxes.

1		one	
2		two	
3		three	
4		four	
5		five	
6		six	
7		seven	
8		eight	
9		nine	
10		ten	

This activity will help your child to practise numbers to 20.

Help by counting the objects, copying the numbers and tracing the number words.

Parents

44

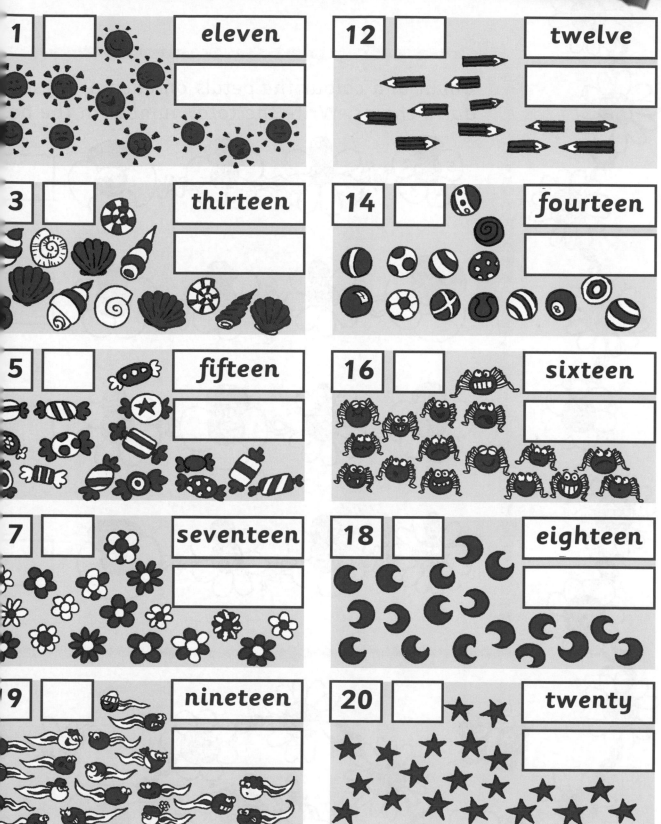

1 | eleven

12 | twelve

3 | thirteen

14 | fourteen

5 | fifteen

16 | sixteen

7 | seventeen

18 | eighteen

9 | nineteen

20 | twenty

7

Counting on

Count and colour the petals on each of these daisy chains. Write the total number in the box:

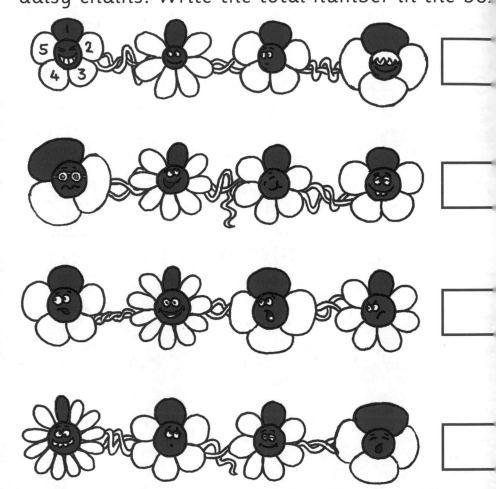

8

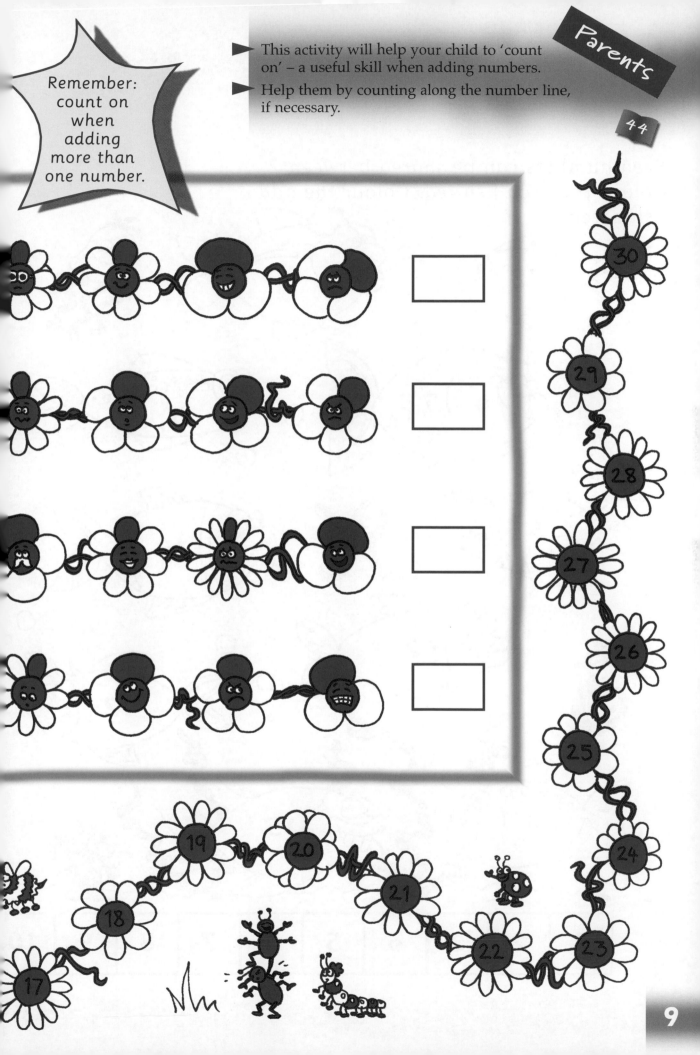

Remember: count on when adding more than one number.

This activity will help your child to 'count on' – a useful skill when adding numbers.

Help them by counting along the number line, if necessary.

Odds and evens

Even numbers can be shared between 2.
Colour the even fish red. Colour the odd
fish green.

18

3

9

7

6

10

2

12

4

15

| 1 | 2 | 3 | 4 | 5 | 6 | 7 | 8 | 9 | 10 |

> This activity will familiarise your child with odd and even numbers.

> They should colour in the numbers on the fish and on the number line in the appropriate colours.

11	12	13	14	15	16	17	18	19	20

Counting in twos

Count in twos to fill in the missing numbers.

1

Now try these.

2

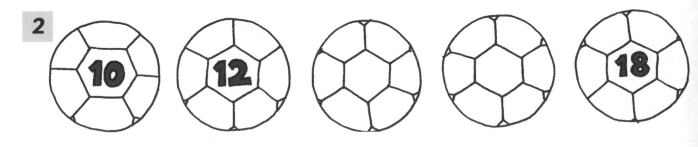

This activity will familiarise your child with counting in twos.

Help them to fill in the missing numbers by referring back to the number line on pages 10–11.

Parents

44

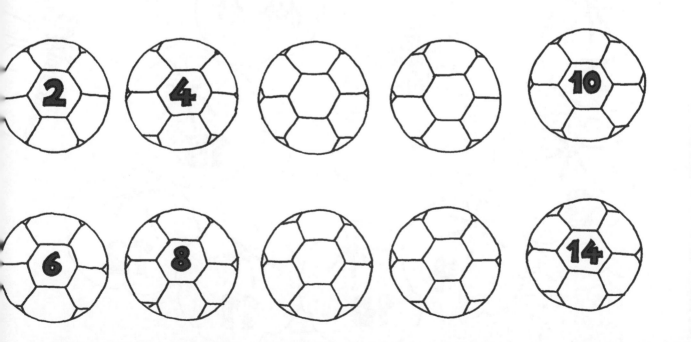

Counting in threes

Frannie the frog jumps 3 lily pads with each hop. Colour the pads she lands on in green.

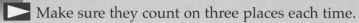

This activity will familiarise your child with counting in threes.

Make sure they count on three places each time.

Parents

45

Counting on again

Draw 2 more cats to make 5 cats.

3 + ☐ = 5

Draw 4 more fish to make 7 fish.

3 + ☐ = 7

Draw 5 more leaves to make 10 leaves.

5 + ☐ = 10

| 1 | 2 | 3 | 4 | 5 | 6 | 7 | 8 | 9 | 10 |

This activity explores addition as 'counting on' from the smaller number to the larger number.

Show your child how to count on using the number line by 'jumping' your finger along.

ow use the number line below to answer these sums.

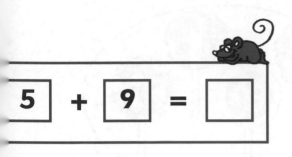

5 + 9 = ☐

12 + 3 = ☐

10 + 5 = ☐

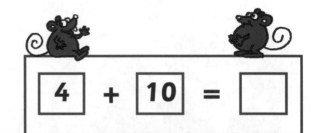

4 + 10 = ☐

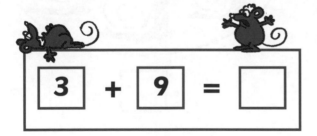

3 + 9 = ☐

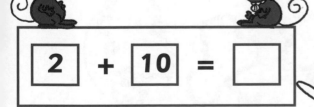

2 + 10 = ☐

Remember, always count on from a number to add the next.

| 11 | 12 | 13 | 14 | 15 | 16 | 17 | 18 | 19 | 20 |

Add as 2 sets

Add these sets of objects.

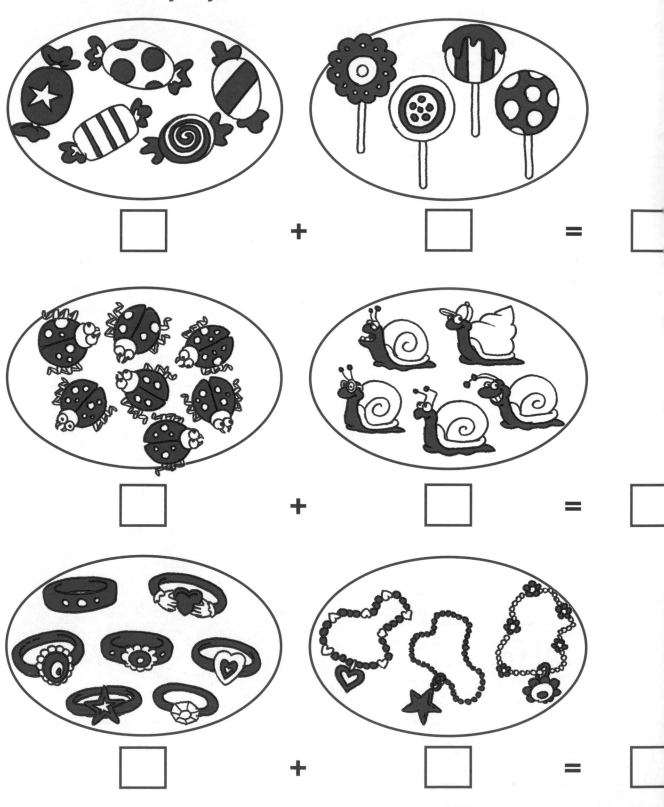

☐ + ☐ = ☐

☐ + ☐ = ☐

☐ + ☐ = ☐

19

Add the large number first

Finish these sums. Start with the larger number and add on the smaller number.

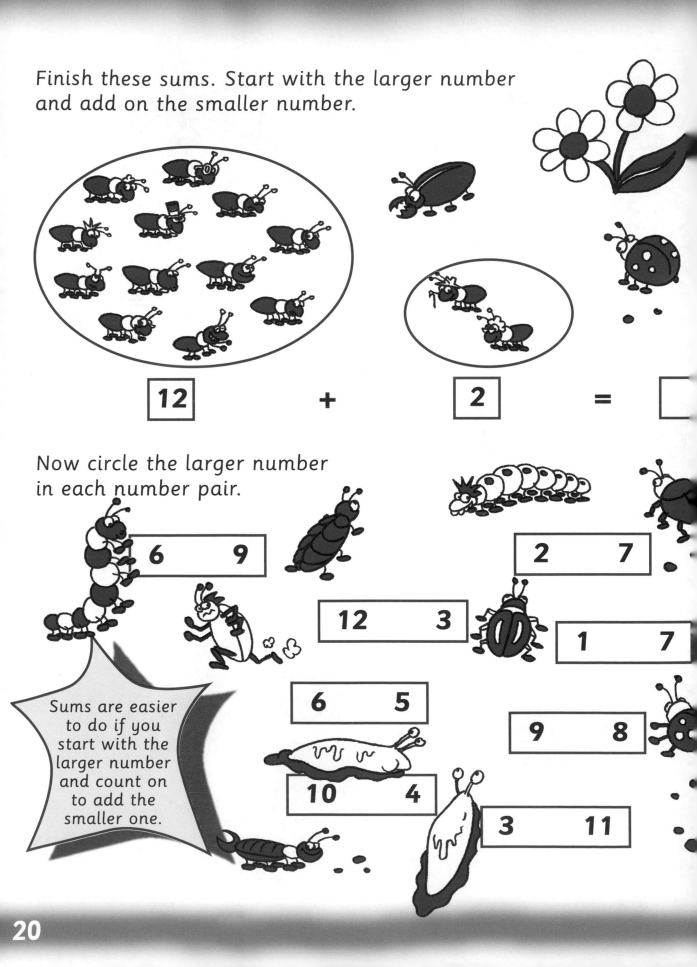

| 12 | + | 2 | = | |

Now circle the larger number in each number pair.

6   9

2   7

12   3

1   7

6   5

9   8

10   4

3   11

Sums are easier to do if you start with the larger number and count on to add the smaller one.

Parents

This activity introduces the mental strategy of putting the larger number first when adding numbers. This will help your child to do sums quickly.

45

It the larger number first, then do the sums!

3 + 9 =

☐ + ☐ = ☐

4 + 8 =

☐ + ☐ = ☐

2 + 10 =

☐ + ☐ = ☐

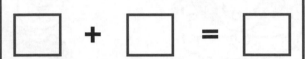

3 + 6 =

☐ + ☐ = ☐

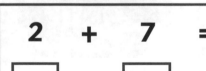

6 + 9 =

☐ + ☐ = ☐

2 + 7 =

☐ + ☐ = ☐

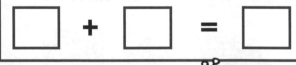

ow write these numbers in order, smallest first.

12	1	5	9	10	3
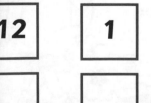					

Adding 3 numbers

Add the numbers on the T-shirts.

> This activity introduces adding together more than two numbers.

> Remind your child to start with the larger number and count on the smaller one.

Add facts to 10

Each gift bag and label added together makes 10.
Write in the missing numbers.

24

This activity shows your child the number combinations that make 10.

Help them to read the number combinations, then join the bow to the correct present to make 10.

Now draw a line to join the bow to the correct gift to make 10.

Adding money

Look at the value of the items
below then complete these sums.

□ + □ = □

□ + □ = □

□ + □ = □

► This activity will show your child how to add money to make a total of up to 20p.

► You might like to use real coins to help them.

Parents

4 6

☐ + ☐ = ☐

☐ + ☐ = ☐

☐ + ☐ = ☐

3p

7p

10p

Lucinda Ladybird

Lucinda Ladybird is hungry and she has eaten some of the aphids. Write how many aphids are left on each leaf. Cross out each aphid as you work.

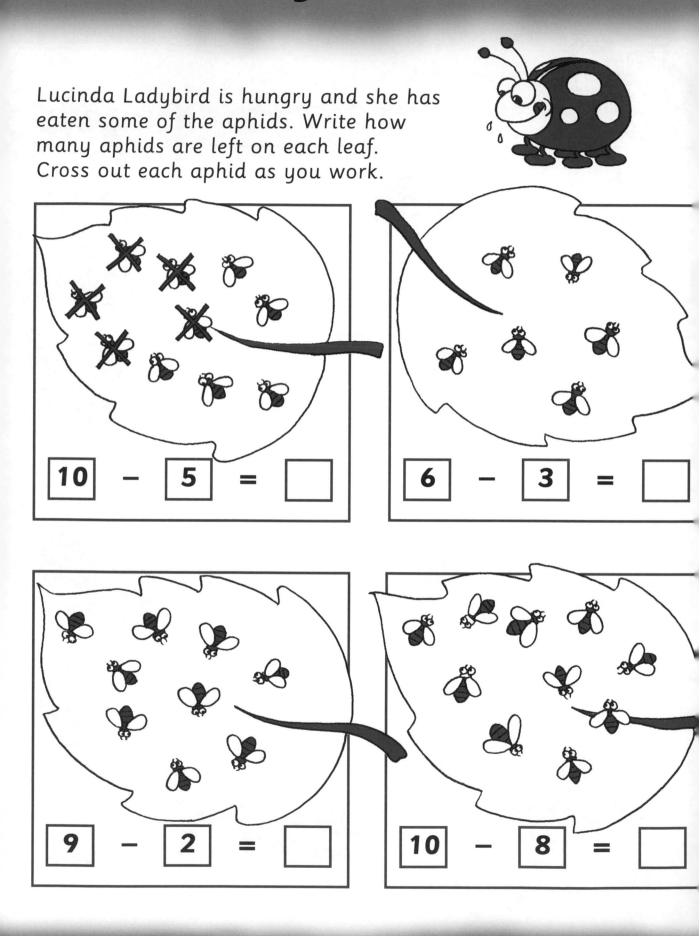

$$10 - 5 = \boxed{}$$

$$6 - 3 = \boxed{}$$

$$9 - 2 = \boxed{}$$

$$10 - 8 = \boxed{}$$

This activity explores subtraction as 'taking away'.

Help your child to count back on the number line (pages 16–17) if they find this difficult.

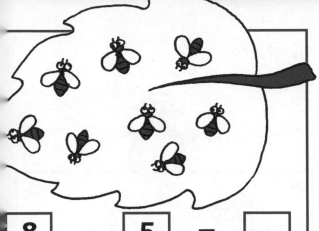

8 − 5 = ☐

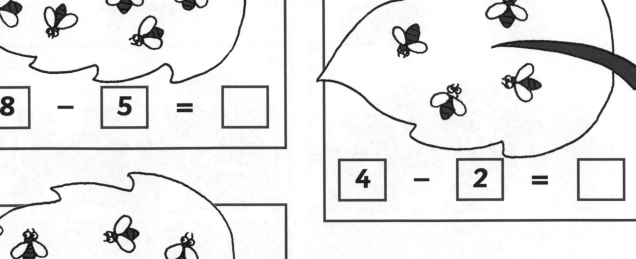

4 − 2 = ☐

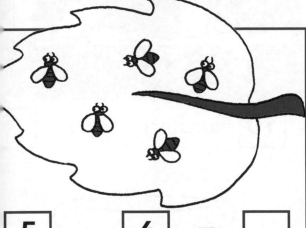

5 − 4 = ☐

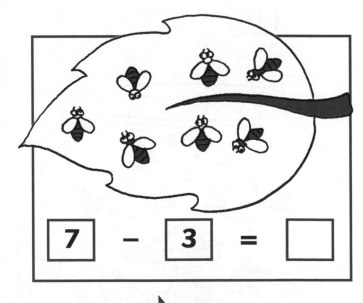

7 − 3 = ☐

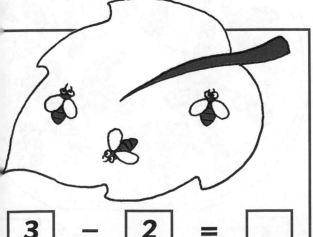

3 − 2 = ☐

Remember to start with the larger number and count back the smaller one!

29

What is the difference?

Find the difference between these numbers.

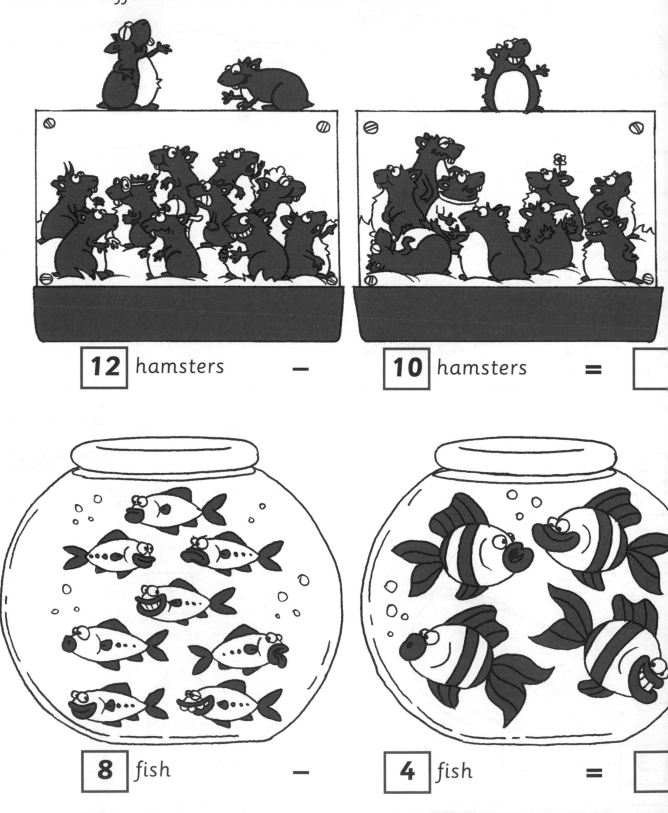

| 12 | hamsters | — | 10 | hamsters | = | |

| 8 | fish | — | 4 | fish | = | |

► This activity shows your child subtraction as the difference between two numbers.

► Use dried pasta to demonstrate each calculation.

Parents

46

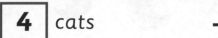 **4** cats   −   **2** cats   =   ☐

3 dogs   −   **1** dog   =   ☐

31

Tens and units

Circle each set of 10 in the pictures. Then write how many tens and units there are.

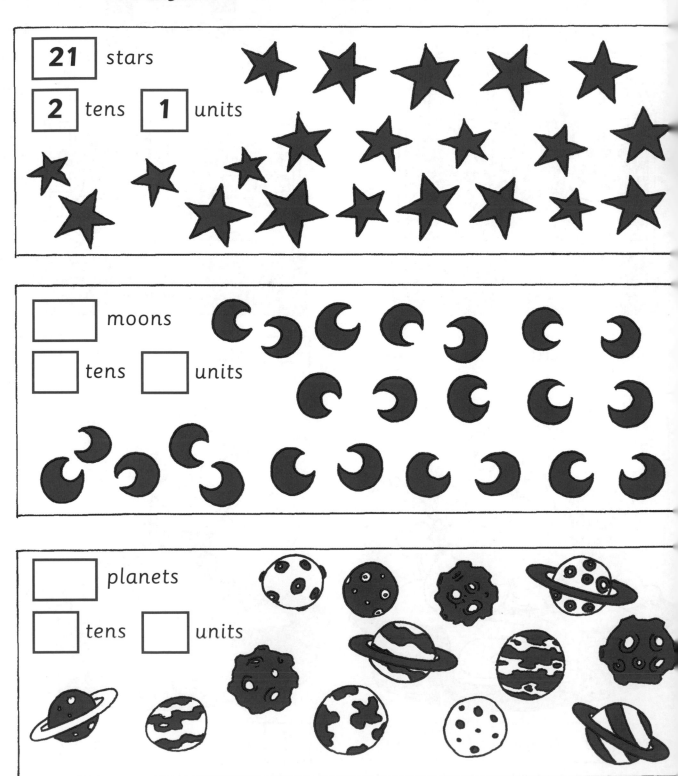

21 stars

2 tens **1** units

moons

tens units

planets

tens units

This activity will help your child to see 2-digit numbers as 'tens' and 'units'.

Help them to draw a circle around each set of 10 that they count, then record the number of tens and units in the boxes.

[ ] spaceships

[ ] tens [ ] units

[ ] aliens

[ ] tens [ ] units

33

Tina's tickets

Tina the Tyrannosaurus has some raffle tickets.
Can you list them in order, smallest first?

Tuesday Night: Randy Ralph!

EXIT

Tina's Tickets

This activity will help your child to order numbers from the smallest to the largest.

Remind them of the number line on page 16, if necessary.

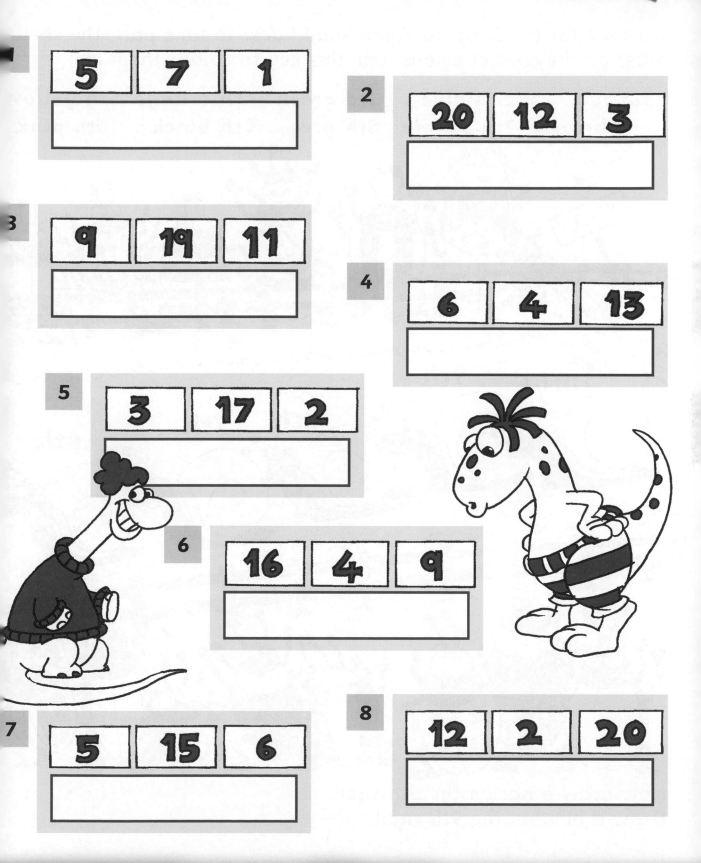

1

| 5 | 7 | 1 |

2

| 20 | 12 | 3 |

3

| 9 | 19 | 11 |

4

| 6 | 4 | 13 |

5

| 3 | 17 | 2 |

6

| 16 | 4 | 9 |

7

| 5 | 15 | 6 |

8

| 12 | 2 | 20 |

35

Snail race

It's time for the Slippery Slime Snail Race! To take part, the shells must be the correct colour. Use this key to colour them in.

1st red	2nd blue	3rd green	4th orange	5th yellow
6th brown	7th purple	8th grey	9th black	10th pink

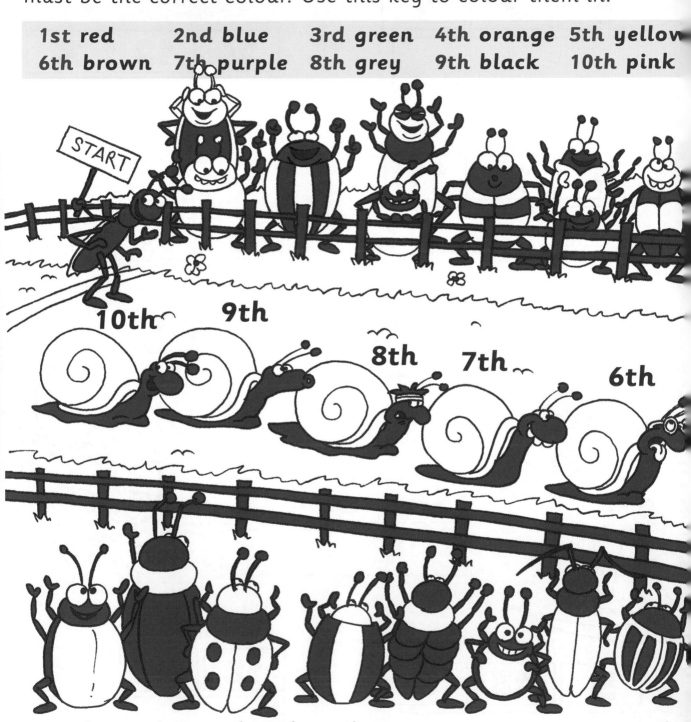

Now draw a hat on the 5th snail.
Draw a bow on the 9th snail.

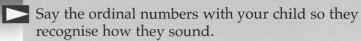

This race will help your child to recognise the order of ordinal numbers – that is 1st, 2nd, 3rd...

Say the ordinal numbers with your child so they recognise how they sound.

Fatima Fairy

Fatima Fairy has a special trick. If she knows one sum,
she can work out three others to make a set.

Look!

$$5 + 4 = 9$$
$$9 - 4 = 5$$
$$4 + 5 = 9$$
$$9 - 5 = 4$$

This activity will show your child the relationship between addition and subtraction.

Point out that all four sums in each set contain the same numbers.

ll in the missing numbers.

$1 + 2 = 3$

$3 - ★ = 1$

$2 + ★ = 3$

$3 - ★ = 2$

$6 + 2 = 8$

$8 - ★ = 6$

$2 + ★ = 8$

$8 - ★ = 2$

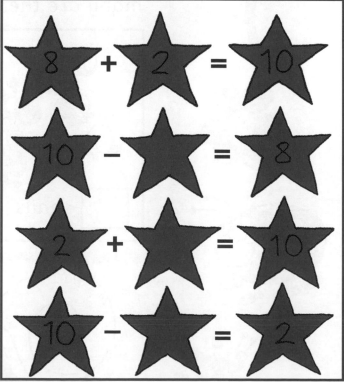

39

Lots of ladybirds

There are 2 ladybirds but 1 runs away. How many are left?

[ ] ladybird

There are 4 spiders but 2 run away. How many are left?

[ ] spiders

There is 1 snail and 4 more come along. How many are there now?

[ ] snails

There are 6 worms and more come along. How many are there now?

[ ] worms

This activity will encourage your child to create number stories, an activity they will be doing at school.

Help them to make up stories about each creature using addition and subtraction.

ake up your own number stories about:

_____

_____

_____

[ ] butterflies

[ ] hedgehogs

_____

_____

_____

[ ] robins

[ ] toads

The sweetshop

gobble choc. bomb: 5p	toffee twists: 8p	truffle bar: 10p	fizzers (each): 2p

How much change will these
children get from 20p if they buy:

Draw the coins.

Rashid spent [   ]

He has [   ] left.

Draw the coins.

Eleanor spent [   ]

She has [   ] left.

42

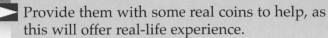

Draw the coins.

Alex spent [ ]

He has [ ] left.

Draw the coins.

Dani spent [ ]

She has [ ] left.

Draw the coins.

Dean spent [ ]

He has [ ] left.

43

Further activities

▶ Extend your child's experience of the number sequence to 20 by counting together up to 20 and back. Take turns to count to 20 leaving out numbers for you or your child to fill in.

▶ *Answers: A. 3, 4, 7, 8, 9, 14, 15, 17, 18.*

B. 2, 3, 5, 6, 8, 9, 10, 14, 15, 17, 18, 20.

6-7

▶ Play a game where you say a number and your child writes the number or the number word. Write the word numbers in pencil, before asking your child to 'overwrite' the words in pen or crayon.

8-9

▶ Encourage your child to count on by counting a series of numbers starting anywhere between 0 and 30 and then stopping, for example at 17, and asking them to continue. You could also take turns saying numbers starting from any point between 0 and 30.

▶ *Answers: numbers of petals: 21, 22, 26, 29, 22, 23, 28, 21.*

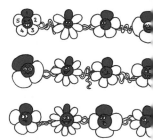

10-11

▶ Talk about 'even' numbers as numbers you can share between 2 exactly with none left over. Try out a series

of numbers and ask your child to predict whether they are even or odd. Help them to recognise the odd and even sequences to 10 by counting together evens: 2 4 6 8 10   odds: 1 3 5 7 9.

12-13

▶ Extend this activity by counting in twos with your child at every opportunity, for example, climbing stairs or taking steps as you count in twos. How far can your child go? Can they see a pattern in the written sequence 0 2 4 6 8 10 12 14 16 18 20?

▶ *Answers: 1. 10, 12. 2. 14, 16. 3. 6, 8. 4. 10, 12.*

Continue to practise this sequence of numbers by making up nonsense rhymes to accompany the numbers, for example,
'3 sit on my knee'
'6 get up to tricks'
'9 ready to dine', and so on.

▶ Try to make rhymes for multiples of 3 up to 30.

▶ *Answers: 3, 6, 9, 12, 15, 18, 21, 24, 27, 30.*

Use real objects to give your child extra practice at this activity. Lay out a line of 20 objects (beads, buttons or sweets) and ask

your child to use the objects to help them to carry out simple additions, such as 8 + 5. They should start from the eighth object and count on 5 more to get a total.

▶ *Answers: 5 + 9 = 14, 12 + 3 = 15, 10 + 5 = 15, 4 + 10 = 14, 3 + 9 = 12, 2 + 10 = 12.*

Extend this activity by laying out small sets of objects (pine cones, shells or acorns) with a piece of card next to each set showing the number represented. For example, three pine cones with '3' written on paper laid next to the set. Give your child a blank square of paper on which to write the answer.

▶ *Answers: 9 sweets, 12 beetles/snails, 10 rings/necklaces, 7 bats/birds, 9 apples/drinks, 5 mice/cheese.*

▶ Make a set of 0–30 number cards (cereal packet card will do). Choose six cards from the pack and ask your child to arrange them in order from smallest to largest. As they become more familiar with the order of the numbers give them more cards, up to 10 at a time, to arrange.

▶ *Answers: 14 ants.*
*Larger numbers: (6 **9**), (2 **7**), (**12** 3), (1 **7**), (**6** 5), (**9** 8), (**10** 4), (3 **11**).*
Sums: 9 + 3 = 12, 8 + 4 = 12, 10 + 2 = 12, 6 + 3 = 9, 9 + 6 = 15, 7 + 2 = 9.
Order: 1, 3, 5, 9, 10, 12.

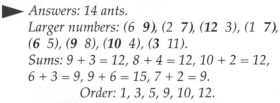

Use groups of objects to practise adding more than three numbers together, for instance, make three piles containing four, five and six objects and ask your child to add them together.

Answers: 10, 8, 12, 6, 11, 8.

Further activities

24-25

▶ Make 11 cards (paper would do) and write these number pairs on the cards, one of the pair on each side of the card: (0, 10) (1, 9) (2, 8) (3, 7) (4, 6) (5, 5) (6, 4) (7, 3) (8, 2) (9, 1) (10, 0).

Your child should look at the number on the card and try to remember the number on the other side of the card. Each card makes a total of 10.

▶ *Answers: 0/10, 1/9, 2/8, 3/7, 4/6, 5/5, 6/4, 7/3, 8/2, 9/1 10/0. Then check your child has joined the correct gift bags and labels.*

26-27

▶ Practise adding with real money. Have ready a quantity of 1p, 2p, 5p and 10p coins for your child to use – either real money or plastic play coins. Use items from the food cupboard, make modelling clay food or use toy food with labels attached to 'buy' things from your child and ask them how much you have spent. Give them a turn at being the customer.

▶ *Answers: 18p, 15p, 15p, 19p, 9p, 13p.*

28-29

▶ Extend this activity by cutting a red ladybird from card or felt or, alternatively, help your child to draw a ladybird and colour it in. Make ten 'aphids' from green modelling clay, or use green sweets. Tell your child different numbers of aphids that the ladybird has eaten, and ask them

to tell you how many are left by physically moving the 'aphids' off the 'ladybird'.

▶ *Answers: 10 − 5 = 5, 6 − 3 = 3, 9 − 2 = 7, 10 − 8 = 2, 8 − 5 = 3, 4 − 2 = 2, 5 − 4 = 1, 7 − 3 = 4, 3 − 2 = 1.*

30-31

▶ Use construction pieces in towers to make a tower of six and a tower of ten. Say 'What is the difference between six and ten?' Count the extra four cubes with your child. Repeat the activity with other numbers.

▶ *Answers: 2 hamsters, 4 fish, 2 cats, 2 dogs.*

32-33

▶ Collect together groups of objects (between 11 and 30). Ask your child to split the objects into groups of 10 and then count how many are left over. Talk to your child about the number of tens and units in a number, for instance, in 23 there are 2 tens and 3 units.

▶ *Answers: 23 moons = 2 tens 3 units,*
13 planets = 1 ten 3 units,
11 spaceships = 1 ten 1 unit,
12 aliens = 1 ten 2 units.

- Make a set of cards numbered 1–20. Shuffle the pile of cards and give your child six cards to put in order. Increase the number of cards each time they have a turn.

- Answers: 1. 1   5   7
            2. 3   12 20

3.	9	11	19
4.	4	6	13
5.	2	3	17
6.	4	9	16
7.	5	6	15
8.	2	12	20

► Extend this activity by using soft toys. Make 'bibs' for the toys from paper marked from 1st–10th. Ask your child to put them in the correct order, then ask them to put a hat on the 9th toy; a scarf on the 6th toy, and so on.

► Make a set of cards showing – + = and the numbers 1–10. Arrange the cards to make a sum, for instance, 1 + 4 = 5. Ask your child to 'read' the sum. Say 'Can you do the sum again in a different order to get back to 1?' Show them how by saying 5 – 4 = 1. Do this for other sums.

► Answers: $3 - 2 = 1$, $2 + 1 = 3$, $3 - 1 = 2$; $8 - 2 = 6$, $2 + 6 = 8$, $8 - 6 = 2$; $7 - 3 = 4$, $3 + 4 = 7$, $7 - 4 = 3$; $10 - 2 = 8$, $2 + 8 = 10$, $10 - 8 = 2$.

► Develop your child's experience of addition and subtraction by making up number stories together about toys and animals.

► Answers: There is 1 ladybird left, 2 spiders left, 5 snails in total, 8 worms in total.

► Play 'shops' again, this time encouraging your child to use 1p, 2p, 5p and 10p coins to make change from 20p.

► Answers: Rashid spent 9p with 11p change, Eleanor spent 12p with 8p change, Alex spent 8p with 12p change, Dean spent 13p with 7p change, Danielle spent 15p with 5p change.

47

Celebration!

You are so clever! Colour the stars to show what you can do!

I can count to 20.

I know odds and evens.

I can add more than two numbers together.

I can handle money up to 20p.